CLASSIC SYMPHONIES
for Timpani

Compiled by
MORRIS GOLDENBERG

Haydn

Mozart

Beethoven

HAL•LEONARD®
CORPORATION
7777 W. BLUEMOUND RD. P.O. BOX 13819 MILWAUKEE, WI 53213

Foreword

This collection of timpani parts is a continuation of a series which began with *CLASSIC OVERTURES for Timpani*. Like its predecessor, this book's pages are reproduced from the standard orchestral editions used by every symphony in the land. The student who studies its contents will become familiar with the appearance of the professional timpanist's library, and will never have to unlearn what he has already accomplished.

As before, the classic symphonies included here were selected because of the special role the timpani part plays in the texture of each composition.

Table of Contents

Symphony No. 94
("Surprise" Symphony)

TIMPANI

Joseph Haydn

in D. G.
MENUETTO
Allegro molto.
tr
Trio.
Men. D. C.
in D.G.
Allegro di molto.
Viol.
L
M
N
O
P
Q
R
dim.

Symphonie Nr. 100.

8

in **G.D.**
FINALE.
Presto.

Symphony No. 101 (*The Clock*)

(London Symphony No. 11)

Timpani

Joseph Haydn

Symphonie № 31.

Timpani.

in **D. A.**

W. A. Mozart, K. V. 297.

Allegro assai.

Andantino tacet.

Symphony No. 34

Timpani (C–G)

TIMPANI

W. A. Mozart, K. 338.

Andante di molto tacet.

FINALE.
Allegro vivace.

18

Symphony No. 35
"Haffner" Symphony

Timpani in **D. A**

W. A. Mozart, K. 385

Allegro con spirito.

Andante tacet.

Symphonie N° 36.

W. A. Mozart. Werk 425.

22

Symphony No. 38 ("Prague" Symphony)
D major
TIMPANI in D. A.

Wolfgang Amadeus Mozart, K. 504

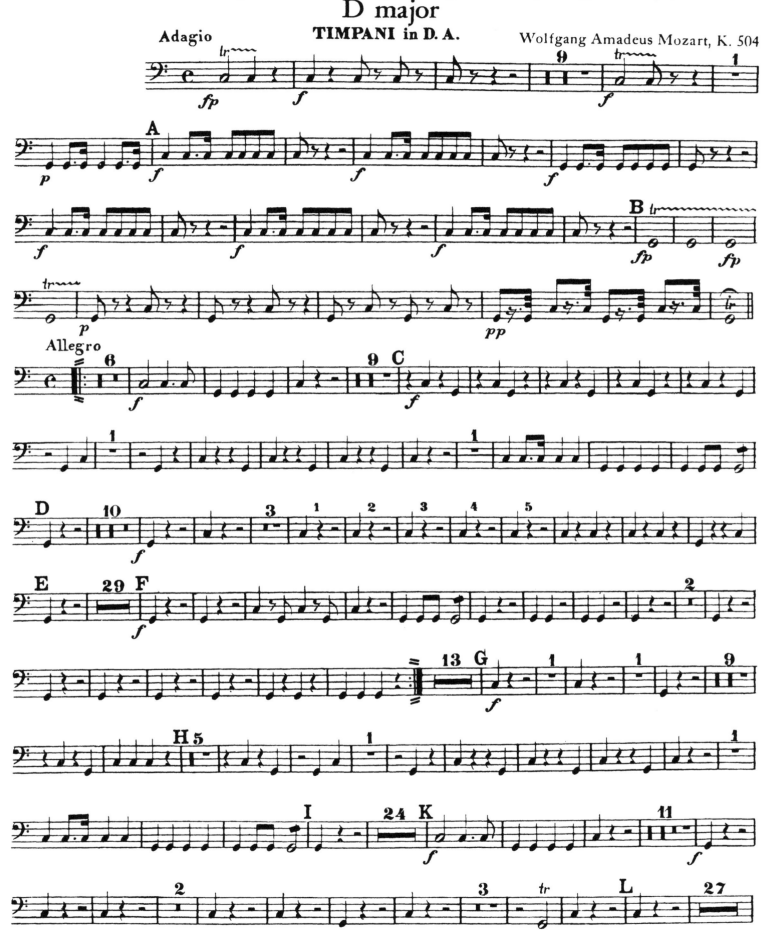

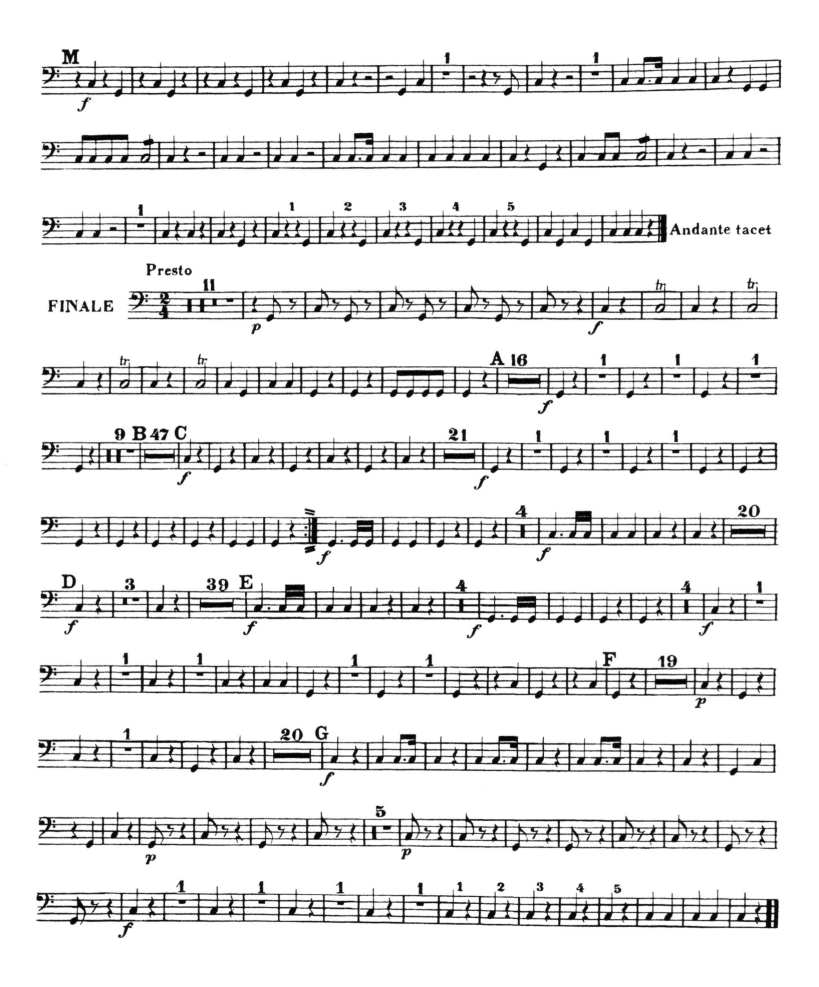

Symphony No. 39

Timpani
Eb–Bb

W. A. Mozart, K. 543.

SYMPHONY No. 41

("Jupiter" Symphony)

TIMPANI in C.G.

Wolfgang Amadeus Mozart (K. 551)

ANDANTE TACET.

28

First Symphony

TIMPANI in C, G

L. van Beethoven, Op. 21

Menuetto.
Allegro molto e vivace. ♩ = 108.

Trio.

Adagio. ♪ = 63.   Allegro molto e vivace. ♩ = 88.

Men. D. C.

Symphony No. 2

Timpani
D–A

L. v. Beethoven, Op. 36.

Larghetto tacet.

Scherzo.

Trio.

Allegro molto.

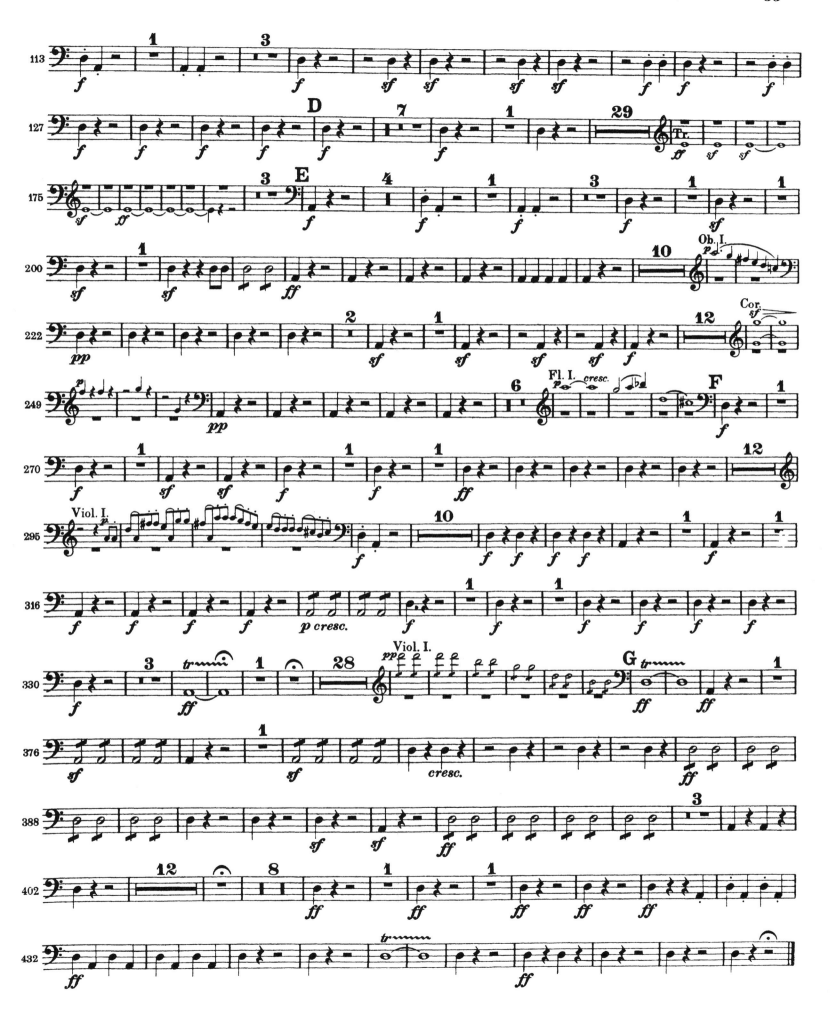

SYMPHONY No. 3
(Eroica)

Timpani

Ludwig van Beethoven, Op. 55

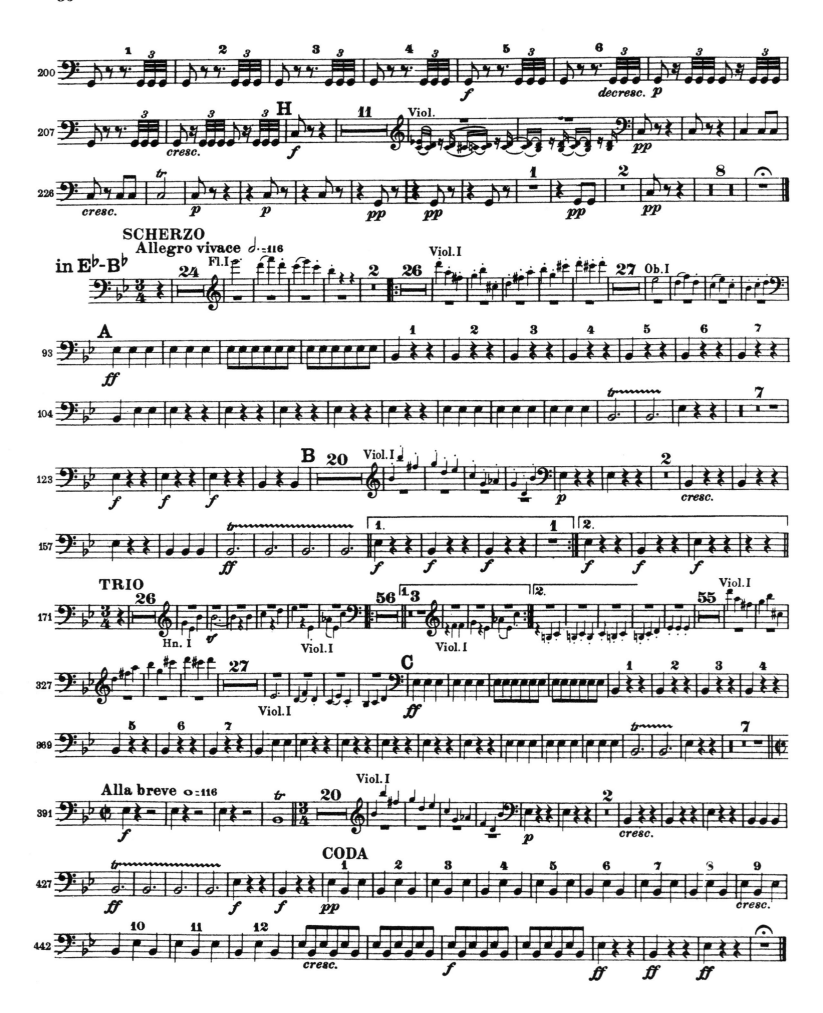

Symphony No. 4

TIMPANI

in B♭ F.

L. van Beethoven, Op. 60

40

Fifth Symphony

TIMPANI in C. G.

L. van Beethoven, Op. 67

44

SYMPHONY No. 6

(Sinfonia Pastorale)

Timpani in C-F

Ludwig van Beethoven, Op. 68

Erwachen heiterer Empfindungen bei der Ankunft auf dem Lande
(*Awakening of Happy Feelings on getting out into the Country*)

Scene am Bach
(*By the Brook-Side*)
Andante molto moto tacet

Allegro ma non troppo tacet

Lustiges Zusammensein der Landleute
(*Merry Gathering of the Country Folk*)

Gewitter. Sturm.
(*Thunderstorm*)

Hirtengesang   Frohe und dankbare Gefühle nach dem Sturm
(*Shepherd's Song   Happy and Thankful Feelings after the Storm*)
Allegretto tacet

Siebente Symphonie

Timpani

in A E

L. van Beethoven, Op. 92

Achte Symphonie.

TIMPANI.

in F. C.

L. van Beethoven, Op. 93.

Allegro vivace e con brio. ♩. = 69.

Allegretto scherzando tacet.

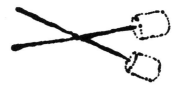

Symphony No. 9

TIMPANI

in **D. A.**

L. van Beethoven, Op. 125

Allegro ma non troppo, un poco maestoso. ♩=88.

60

62